ADELE
FOR BEGINNING PIANO SOLO

Cover photo © Pictorial Press Ltd / Alamy

ISBN 978-1-4950-5883-7

HAL•LEONARD®
CORPORATION

7777 W. BLUEMOUND RD. P.O. BOX 13819 MILWAUKEE, WI 53213

For all works contained herein:
Unauthorized copying, arranging, adapting, recording, Internet posting, public performance,
or other distribution of the printed music in this publication is an infringement of copyright.
Infringers are liable under the law.

Visit Hal Leonard Online at
www.halleonard.com

ALL I ASK

Words and Music by ADELE ADKINS,
PHILIP LAWRENCE, BRUNO MARS
and CHRIS BROWN

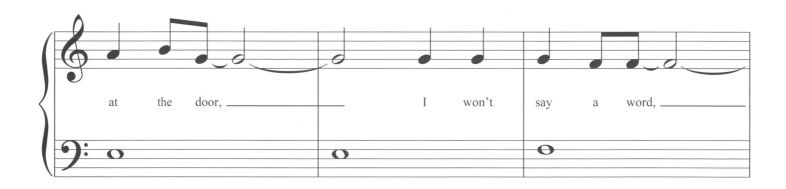

Copyright © 2015 MELTED STONE PUBLISHING LTD., ZZR MUSIC LLC, BMG RIGHTS MANAGEMENT (US) LLC, MARS FORCE MUSIC,
WB MUSIC CORP., THOU ART THE HUNGER, WESTSIDE INDEPENDENT MUSIC PUBLISHING LLC and LATE 80'S MUSIC
This arrangement Copyright © 2016 MELTED STONE PUBLISHING LTD., ZZR MUSIC LLC, BMG RIGHTS MANAGEMENT (US) LLC,
MARS FORCE MUSIC, WB MUSIC CORP., THOU ART THE HUNGER, WESTSIDE INDEPENDENT MUSIC PUBLISHING LLC and LATE 80'S MUSIC
All Rights for MELTED STONE PUBLISHING LTD. in the U.S. and Canada Administered by UNIVERSAL - SONGS OF POLYGRAM INTERNATIONAL, INC.
All Rights for ZZR MUSIC LLC Administered by UNIVERSAL MUSIC CORP.
All Rights for MARS FORCE MUSIC Administered by BMG RIGHTS MANAGEMENT (US) LLC
All Rights for THOU ART THE HUNGER Administered by WB MUSIC CORP.
All Rights for THOU ART THE HUNGER and LATE 80'S MUSIC Administered by WESTSIDE INDEPENDENT MUSIC PUBLISHING LLC
All Rights Reserved   Used by Permission

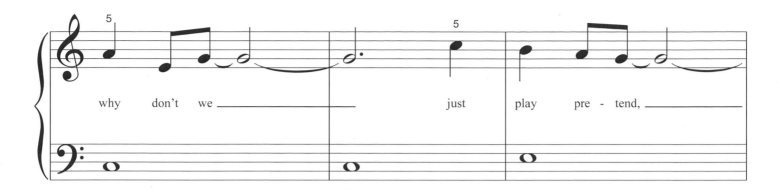

why don't we _____ just play pre - tend, _____

_____ like we're not scared of what is com - ing next, or

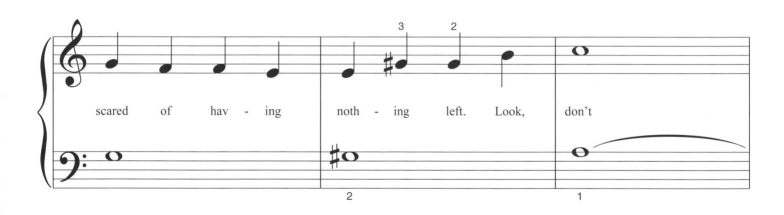

scared of hav - ing noth - ing left. Look, don't

get me wrong, I know there is no to - mor -

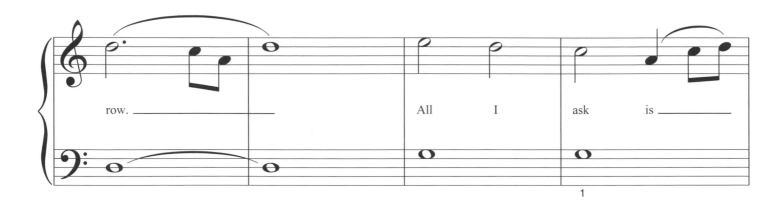

row. All I ask is

if this is my last night with

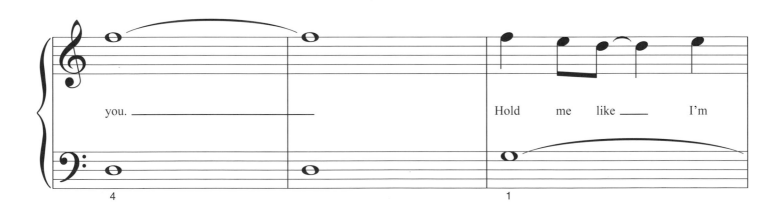

you. Hold me like I'm

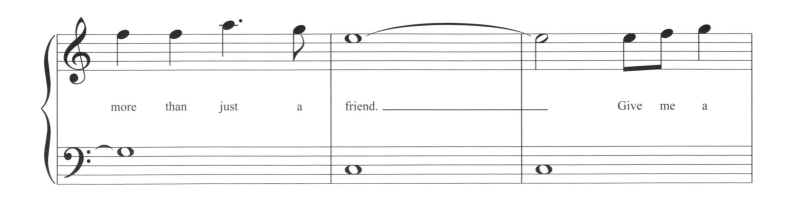

more than just a friend. Give me a

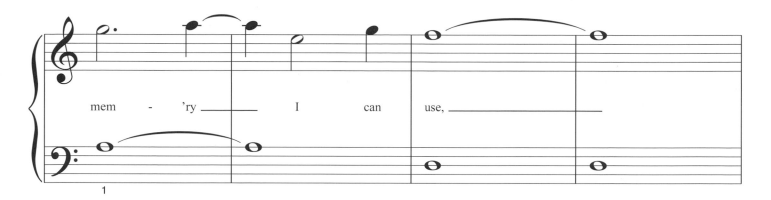

mem - 'ry _____ I can use, _____

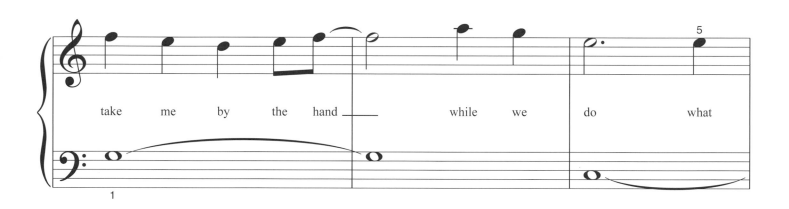

take me by the hand _____ while we do what

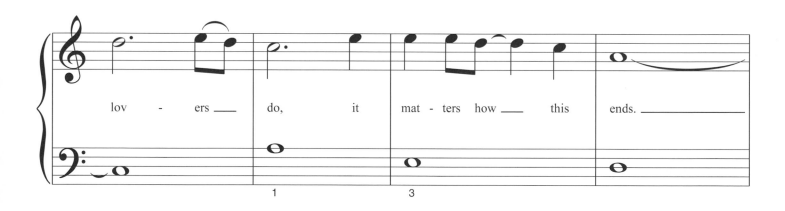

lov - ers _____ do, it mat - ters how _____ this ends. _____

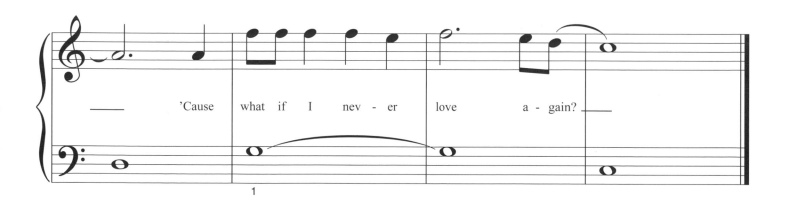

_____ 'Cause what if I nev - er love a - gain? _____

CHASING PAVEMENTS

Words and Music by ADELE ADKINS
and FRANCIS EG WHITE

Moderately slow

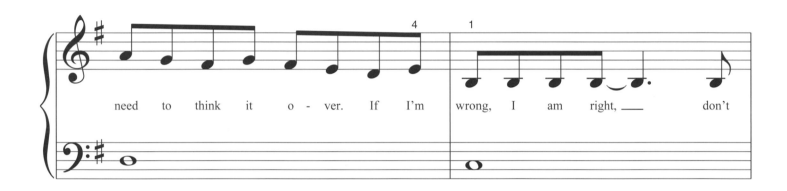

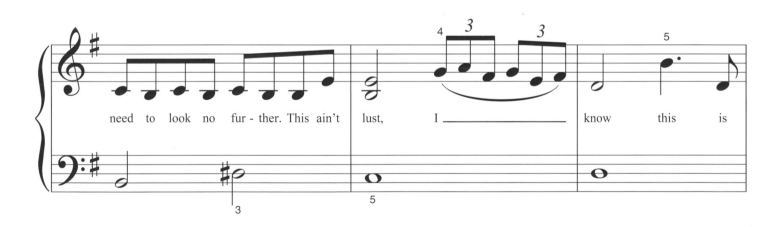

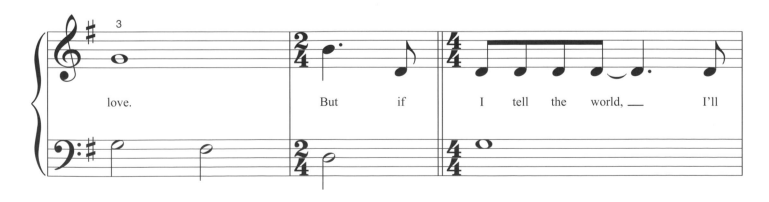

Copyright © 2008 MELTED STONE PUBLISHING LTD. and UNIVERSAL MUSIC PUBLISHING LTD.
This arrangement Copyright © 2016 MELTED STONE PUBLISHING LTD. and UNIVERSAL MUSIC PUBLISHING LTD.
All Rights in the U.S. and Canada Controlled and Administered by UNIVERSAL - SONGS OF POLYGRAM INTERNATIONAL, INC.
All Rights Reserved   Used by Permission

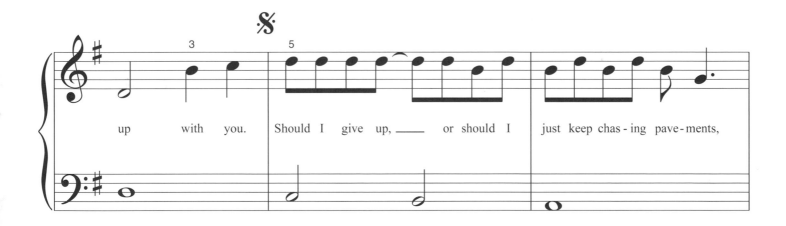

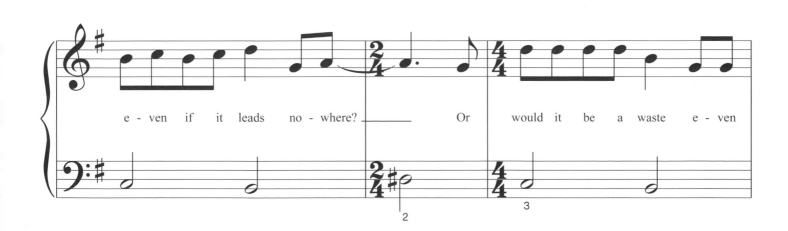

if I knew my place? Should I leave it there? ___ Should I give up, ___ or should I

just keep chas - ing pave-ments, e - ven if it leads no - where?

Yeah. ___ Should I give up, ___ or should I just keep chas - ing pave - ments, e - ven

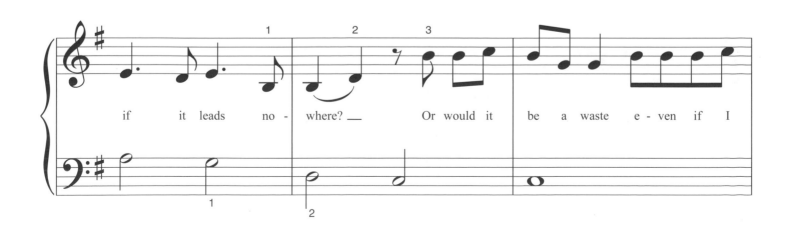

if it leads no - where? ___ Or would it be a waste e - ven if I

knew my place? Should I leave it there? Should I _____ give up, or should I

just keep on chas - ing pave - ments? Should I

D.S. al Coda

just keep on chas - ing pave - ments? _

CODA

leads no - where? _____

HELLO

Words and Music by ADELE ADKINS
and GREG KURSTIN

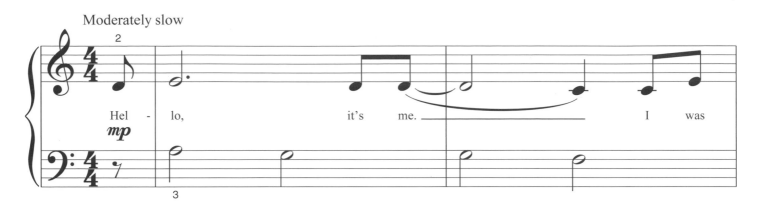

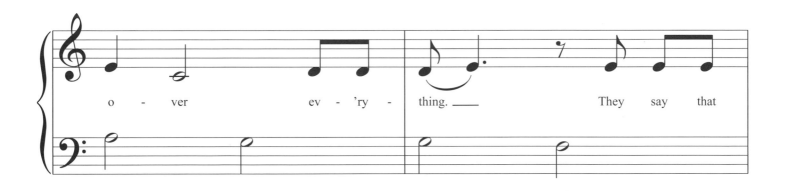

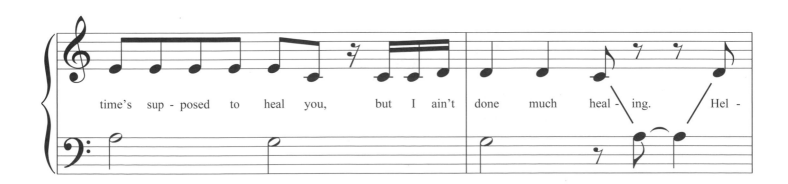

Copyright © 2015 MELTED STONE PUBLISHING LTD., EMI APRIL MUSIC INC. and KURSTIN MUSIC
This arrangement Copyright © 2016 MELTED STONE PUBLISHING LTD., EMI APRIL MUSIC INC. and KURSTIN MUSIC
All Rights for MELTED STONE PUBLISHING LTD. in the U.S. and Canada Administered by UNIVERSAL - SONGS OF POLYGRAM INTERNATIONAL, INC.
All Rights for EMI APRIL MUSIC INC. and KURSTIN MUSIC Administered by SONY/ATV MUSIC PUBLISHING LLC, 424 Church Street, Suite 1200, Nashville, TN 37219
All Rights Reserved   Used by Permission

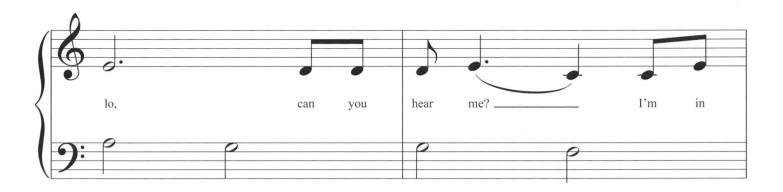

lo, can you hear me? _____ I'm in

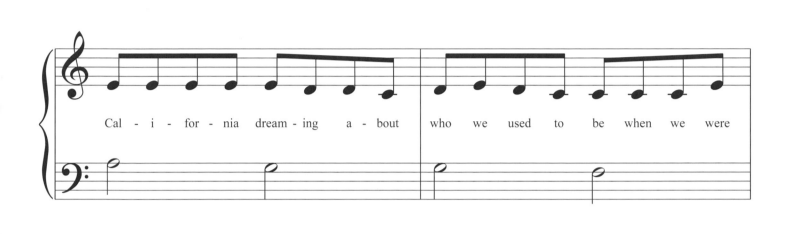

Cal - i - for - nia dream - ing a - bout who we used to be when we were

young - er and free. _____ I've for -

got - ten how it felt be - fore the world fell at our feet. There's such a

dif - f'rence be - tween ___ us, ___ and a mil - li - on ___ miles. ___

____. Hel - lo from the oth - er side. _____ I

must have called a thou - sand times _____ to tell you ___

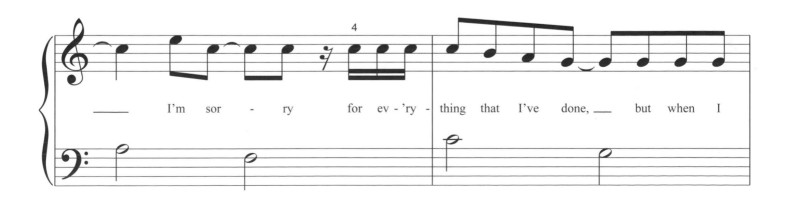

___ I'm sor - ry for ev - 'ry - thing that I've done, ___ but when I

call you nev - er seem to be home. __ Hel - lo from the out - side. __

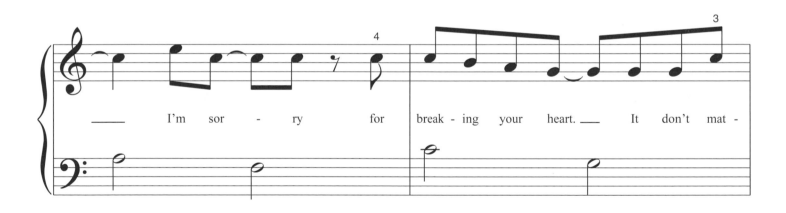

_____ At least I can say that I've tried _____ to tell you __

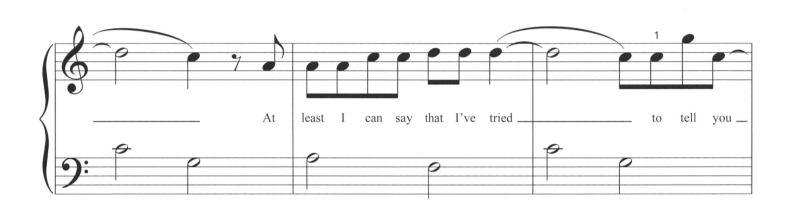

__ I'm sor - ry for break - ing your heart. __ It don't mat -

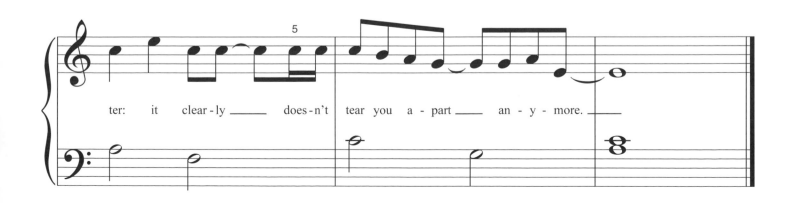

ter: it clear - ly _____ does - n't tear you a - part ___ an - y - more. ___

ROLLING IN THE DEEP

Words and Music by ADELE ADKINS
and PAUL EPWORTH

Soul groove

There's a fire _____ start-ing in my heart, reach-ing a fe-ver pitch and

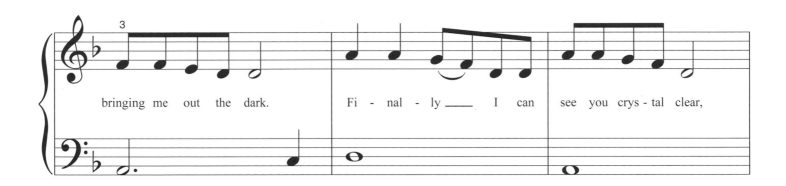

bringing me out the dark. Fi - nal-ly _____ I can see you crys-tal clear,

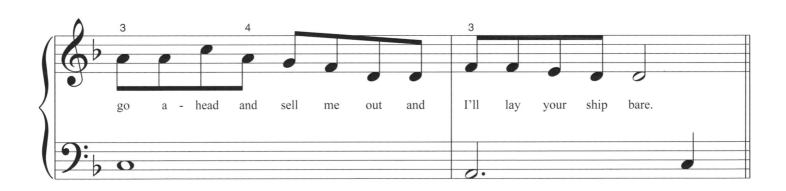

go a-head and sell me out and I'll lay your ship bare.

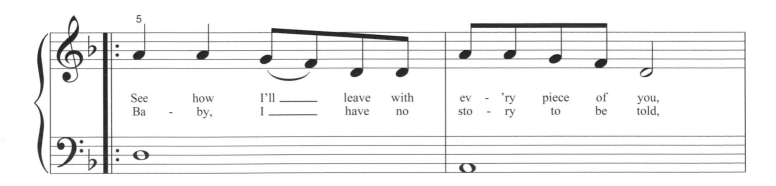

See how I'll _____ leave with ev-'ry piece of you,
Ba - by, I _____ have no sto - ry to be told,

Copyright © 2010, 2011 MELTED STONE PUBLISHING LTD. and EMI MUSIC PUBLISHING LTD.
This arrangement Copyright © 2016 MELTED STONE PUBLISHING LTD. and EMI MUSIC PUBLISHING LTD.
All Rights for MELTED STONE PUBLISHING LTD. in the U.S. and Canada Controlled and Administered by UNIVERSAL - SONGS OF POLYGRAM INTERNATIONAL, INC.
All Rights for EMI MUSIC PUBLISHING LTD. Administered by SONY/ATV MUSIC PUBLISHING LLC, 424 Church Street, Suite 1200, Nashville, TN 37219
All Rights Reserved Used by Permission

don't un - der - es - ti - mate the things that I will do.
I've heard ___ one on you. I'm gonna make your head burn.

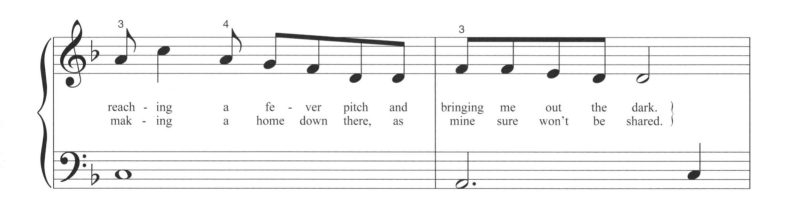

There's a fire ___ start - ing in my heart,
Think of me in the depths of your des - pair,

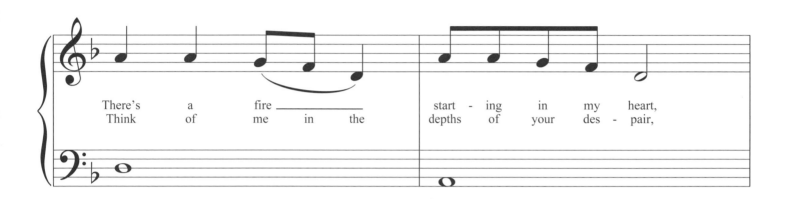

reach - ing a fe - ver pitch and bringing me out the dark.
mak - ing a home down there, as mine sure won't be shared.

The scars of your ___ love re - mind me

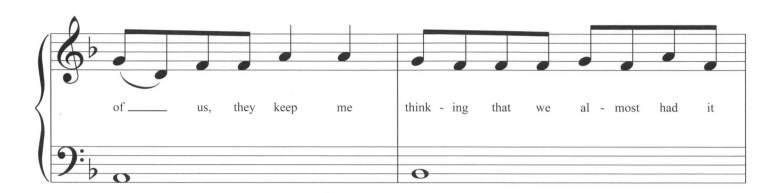

of _____ us, they keep me think - ing that we al - most had it

all. The scars of your _____ love, they leave me

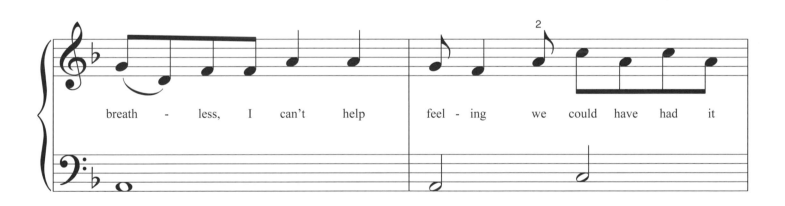

breath - less, I can't help feel - ing we could have had it

all, _____ roll - ing in the deep. _____

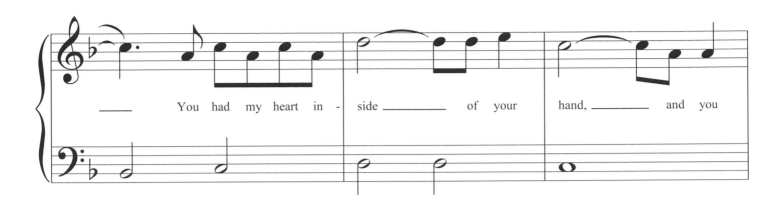

You had my heart in - side _____ of your hand, _____ and you

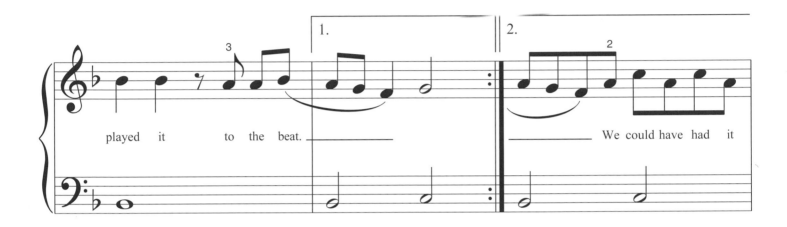

played it to the beat. _____ _____ We could have had it

all. _____ _____ Roll - ing in the deep. _____

_____ You had my heart in - side _____ of your hand, _____ and you

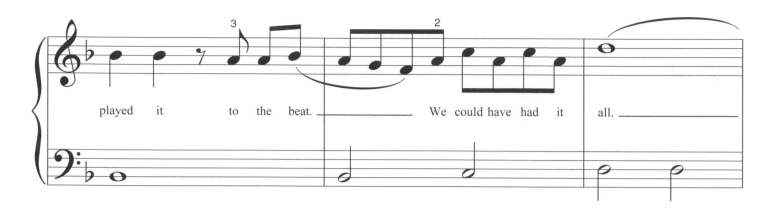

played it to the beat. _____ We could have had it all. _____

_____ Roll - ing in the deep. _____ You had my heart in -

side _____ of your hand, _____ but you played _

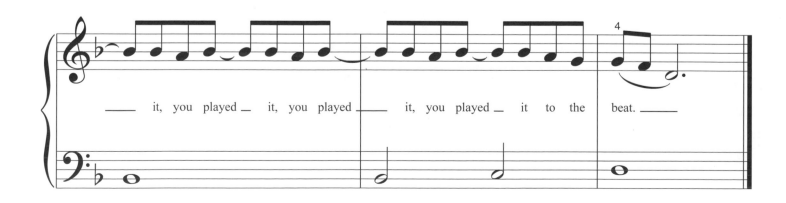

_ it, you played _ it, you played _ it, you played _ it to the beat. _____

REMEDY

Words and Music by ADELE ADKINS
and RYAN TEDDER

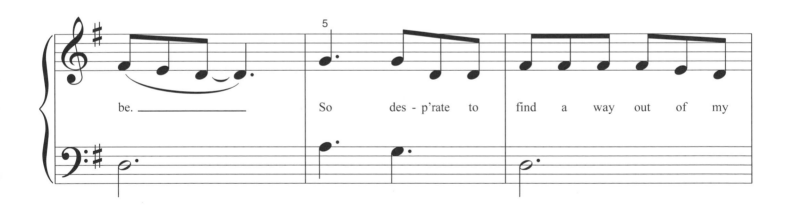

Copyright © 2015 MELTED STONE PUBLISHING LTD. and WRITE ME A SONG PUBLISHING
This arrangement Copyright © 2016 MELTED STONE PUBLISHING LTD. and WRITE ME A SONG PUBLISHING
All Rights for MELTED STONE PUBLISHING LTD. in the U.S. and Canada Administered by UNIVERSAL - SONGS OF POLYGRAM INTERNATIONAL, INC.
All Rights for WRITE ME A SONG PUBLISHING Administered Worldwide by KOBALT MUSIC GROUP LTD.
All Rights Reserved   Used by Permission

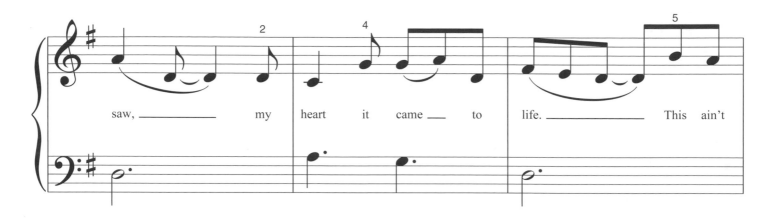

saw, _____ my heart it came ___ to life. _____ This ain't

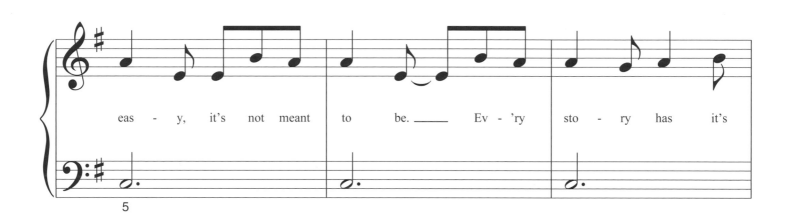

eas - y, it's not meant to be. ___ Ev - 'ry sto - ry has it's

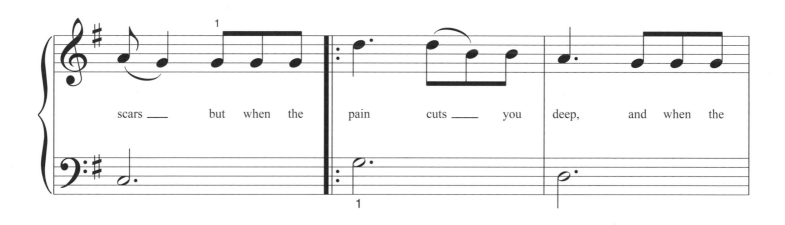

scars ___ but when the pain cuts ___ you deep, and when the

night keeps you from sleep - ing, ___ just look and you will see that I ___ will

be your rem - e - dy. _____ When the world seems so cruel _____ and your

heart makes you feel like a fool, _____ I prom - ise you will

see that I ___ will be, I ___ will be your rem - e - dy. _____

1.

2.

When the

SET FIRE TO THE RAIN

Words and Music by ADELE ADKINS
and FRASER SMITH

Pop Rock

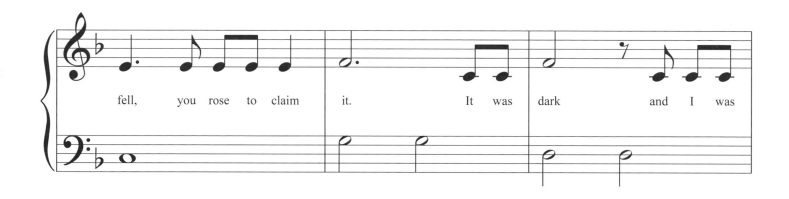

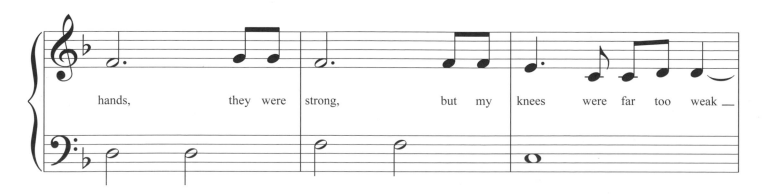

Copyright © 2010, 2011 MELTED STONE PUBLISHING LTD. and CHRYSALIS MUSIC LTD.
This arrangement Copyright © 2016 MELTED STONE PUBLISHING LTD. and CHRYSALIS MUSIC LTD.
All Rights for MELTED STONE PUBLISHING LTD. in the U.S. and Canada Controlled and Administered by UNIVERSAL - SONGS OF POLYGRAM INTERNATIONAL, INC.
All Rights for CHRYSALIS MUSIC LTD. Administered by BMG RIGHTS MANAGEMENT (US) LLC
All Rights Reserved Used by Permission

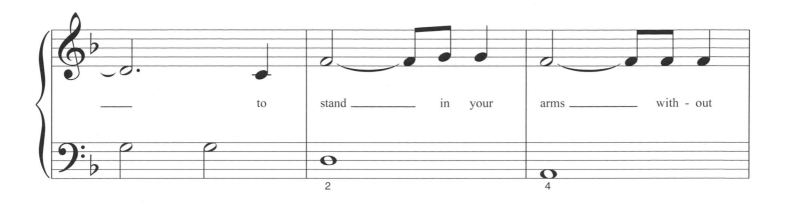

to stand _____ in your arms _____ with - out

fall - ing to your feet. _____ But there's a side to you that I

nev - er knew, nev - er knew. All the things you'd say, they were

nev - er true, nev - er true. And the games you'd play, you would

al - ways win, al - ways win. _____ But I set

fire _____ to the rain, watched it pour as I touched your face. __

_____ Well, it burned __ while I cried, __ 'cause I heard __

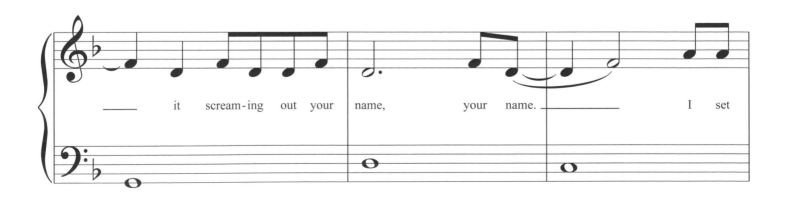

__ it scream-ing out your name, your name. __ _____ I set

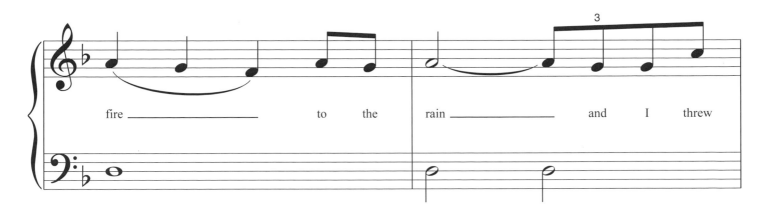

fire _____ to the   rain _____ and I threw

us _____ in - to the flames. _____   Well, I felt _____

To Coda ⊕

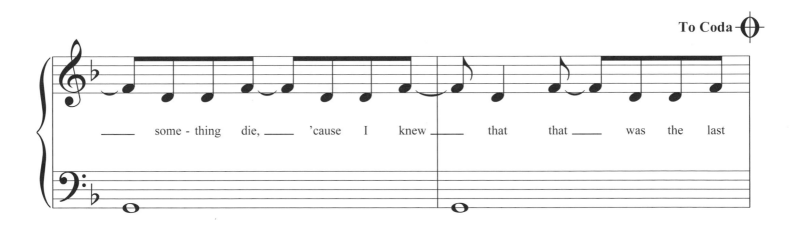

_____ some - thing die, _____ 'cause I knew _____ that that _____ was the last

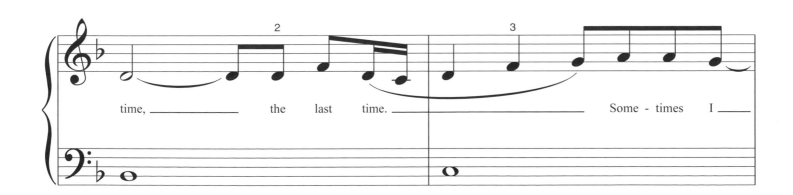

time, _____ the last time. _____   Some - times I _____

wake up by the door. _____ That heart you caught must be wait - ing

for her. _____ E - ven now, when we're al - read - y o - ver, _____ I can't

D.S. al Coda

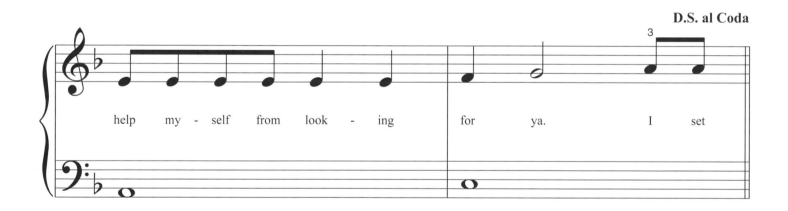

help my - self from look - ing for ya. I set

CODA

time, _____ the last time. _____ (Let it burn.) _____

SKYFALL
from the Motion Picture SKYFALL

Words and Music by ADELE ADKINS
and PAUL EPWORTH

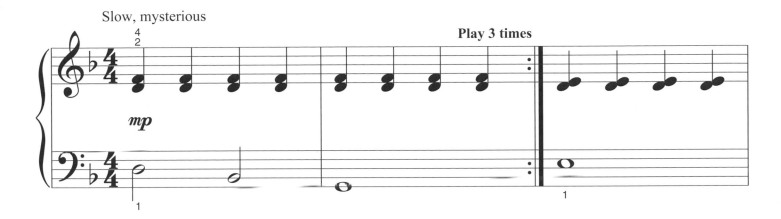

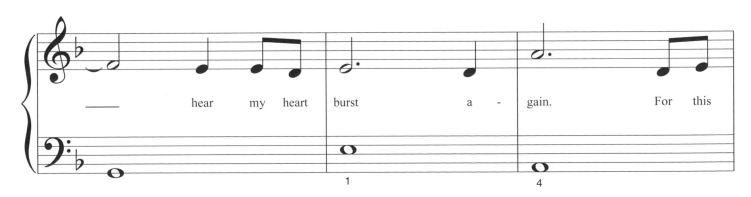

Copyright © 2012 MELTED STONE PUBLISHING LTD. and EMI MUSIC PUBLISHING LTD.
This arrangement Copyright © 2016 MELTED STONE PUBLISHING LTD. and EMI MUSIC PUBLISHING LTD.
All Rights for MELTED STONE PUBLISHING LTD. in the U.S. and Canada Controlled and Administered by UNIVERSAL - SONGS OF POLYGRAM INTERNATIONAL, INC.
All Rights for EMI MUSIC PUBLISHING LTD. Administered by SONY/ATV MUSIC PUBLISHING LLC, 424 Church Street, Suite 1200, Nashville, TN 37219
All Rights Reserved   Used by Permission

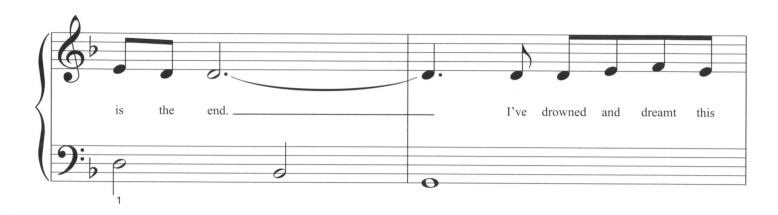

all to - geth - er. Let the sky fall. When it

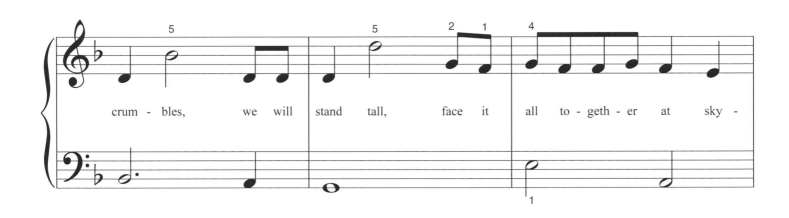

crum - bles, we will stand tall, face it all to - geth - er at sky -

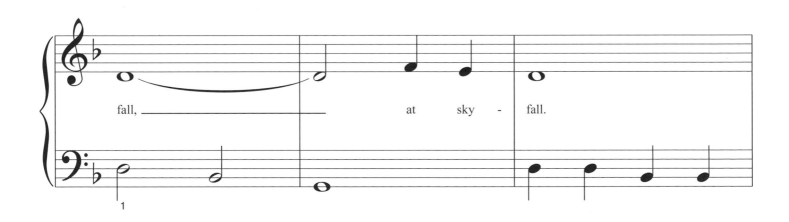

fall, _____ at sky - fall.

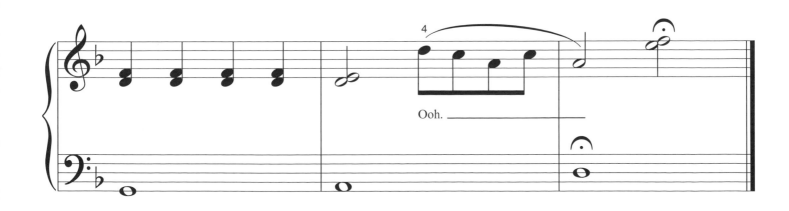

Ooh. _____

TURNING TABLES

Words and Music by ADELE ADKINS
and RYAN TEDDER

Moderate Ballad

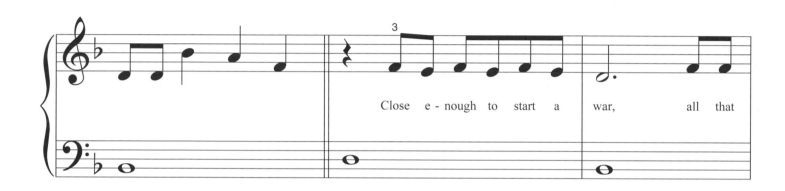

Close e - nough to start a war, all that

I have _____ is on the floor.

God on - ly knows what we're fight - ing for, all that

Copyright © 2011 MELTED STONE PUBLISHING LTD. and WRITE 2 LIVE PUBLISHING
This arrangement Copyright © 2016 MELTED STONE PUBLISHING LTD. and WRITE 2 LIVE PUBLISHING
All Rights for MELTED STONE PUBLISHING LTD. in the U.S. and Canada Controlled and Administered by UNIVERSAL - SONGS OF POLYGRAM INTERNATIONAL, INC.
All Rights for WRITE 2 LIVE PUBLISHING Administered by KOBALT MUSIC PUBLISHING AMERICA, INC.
All Rights Reserved   Used by Permission

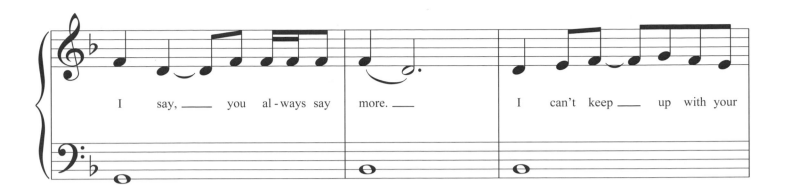

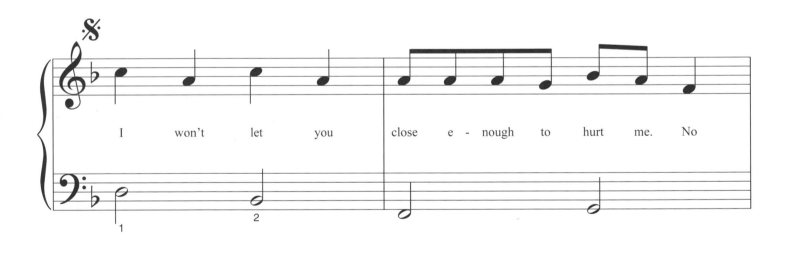

give you — what you think you gave me. ____ It's time to

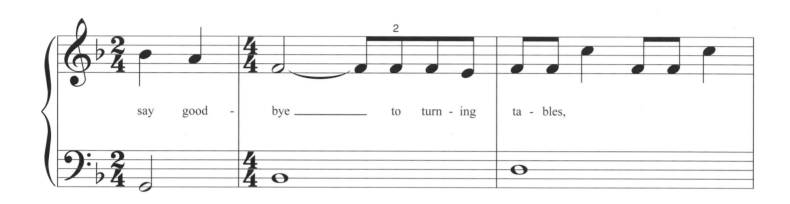

say good - bye ____ to turn - ing ta - bles,

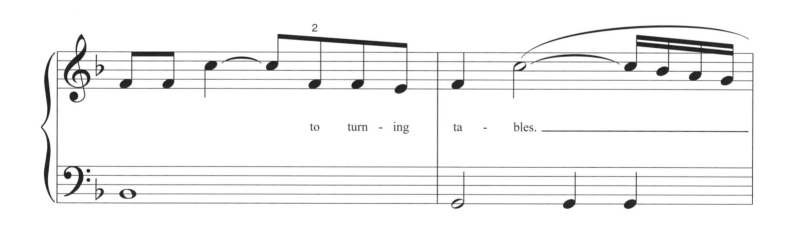

to turn - ing ta - bles. ____

To Coda

____ Next time, I'll __ be brav - er, I'll be my __ own sav - ior

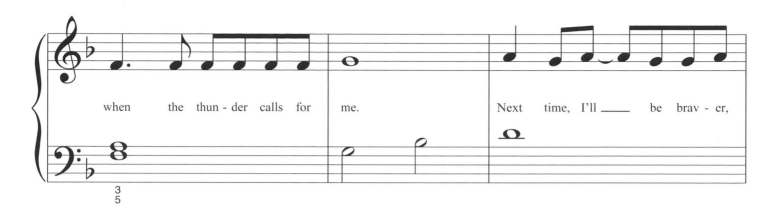

when   the   thun - der calls for   me.   Next   time, I'll ___ be   brav - er,

D.S. al Coda

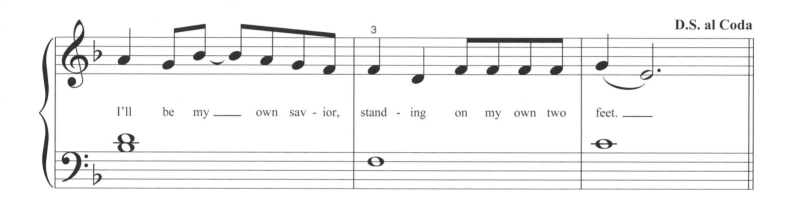

I'll   be   my ___ own sav - ior,   stand - ing   on   my own two   feet. ___

CODA

WHEN WE WERE YOUNG

Words and Music by ADELE ADKINS
and TOBIAS JESSO JR.

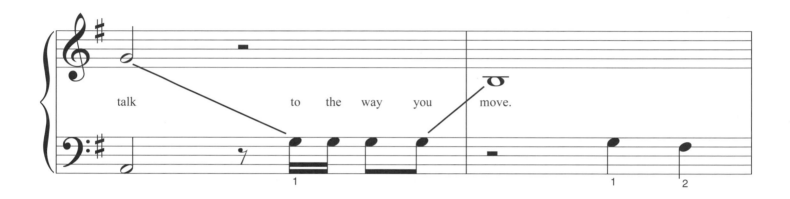

Copyright © 2015 MELTED STONE PUBLISHING LTD. and TOBIAS JESSO, JR.
This arrangement Copyright © 2016 MELTED STONE PUBLISHING LTD. and TOBIAS JESSO, JR.
All Rights for MELTED STONE PUBLISHING LTD. in the U.S. and Canada Administered by UNIVERSAL - SONGS OF POLYGRAM INTERNATIONAL, INC.
All Rights for TOBIAS JESSO, JR. Administered by SONGS OF UNIVERSAL, INC.
All Rights Reserved   Used by Permission

But if by chance you're here a - lone, can I have a

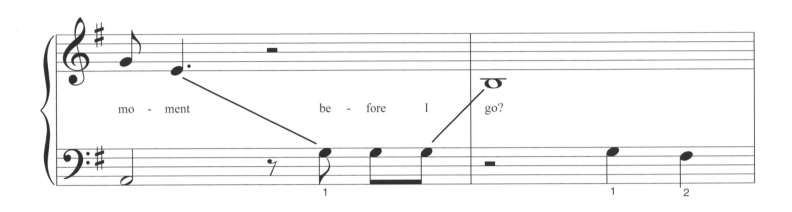

mo - ment be - fore I go?

'Cause I've been by my - self all night long, hop - ing you're

some - one I used to know. You look like a

mov - ie, you sound like a song; my God, this re -

minds me of when we were young. Let me

pho - to - graph you in this light, in case it is the last time that we

might be ex - act - ly like we were be - fore we re - al - ized we were

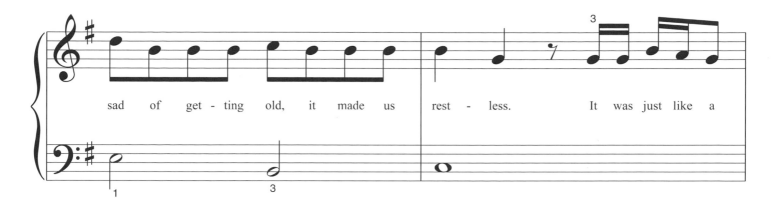

sad of get - ting old, it made us rest - less. It was just like a

mov - ie, it was just like a song. When

we were young, when we were young, when we were young, when we

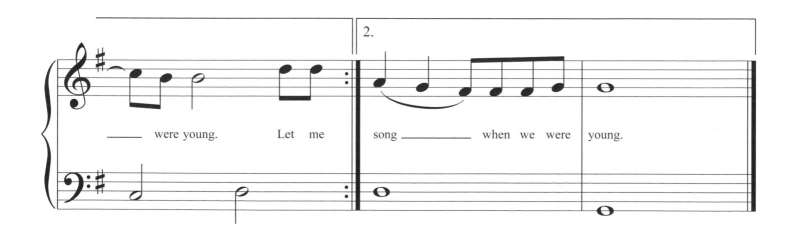

were young. Let me song when we were young.

SOMEONE LIKE YOU

Words and Music by ADELE ADKINS
and DAN WILSON

Moderately slow

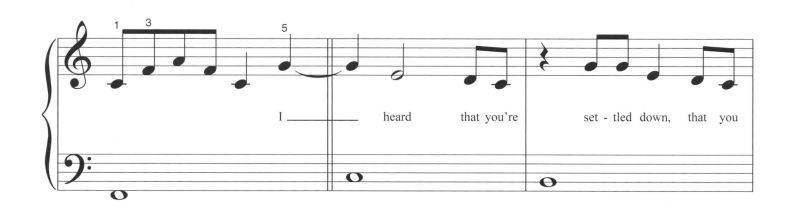

Copyright © 2011 MELTED STONE PUBLISHING LTD., BMG MONARCH and SUGAR LAKE MUSIC
This arrangement Copyright © 2016 MELTED STONE PUBLISHING LTD., BMG MONARCH and SUGAR LAKE MUSIC
All Rights for MELTED STONE PUBLISHING LTD. in the U.S. and Canada Controlled and Administered by UNIVERSAL - SONGS OF POLYGRAM INTERNATIONAL, INC.
All Rights for BMG MONARCH and SUGAR LAKE MUSIC Administered by BMG RIGHTS MANAGEMENT (US) LLC
All Rights Reserved   Used by Permission

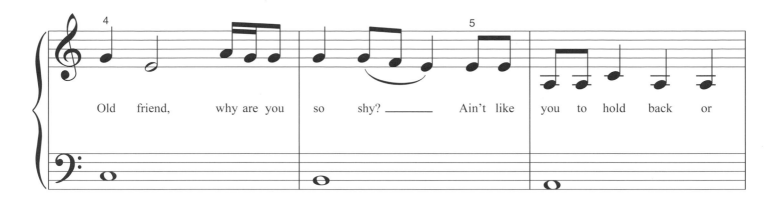

Old friend, why are you so shy? _____ Ain't like you to hold back or

hide from the light.

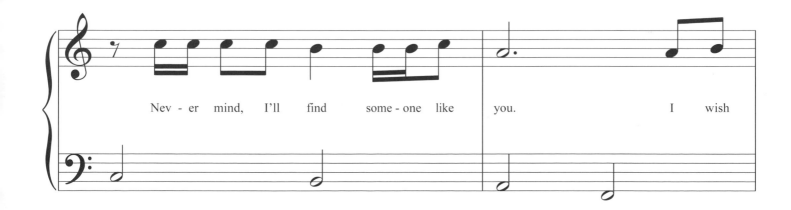

Nev - er mind, I'll find some - one like you. I wish

noth - ing but the best for ___ you, too. Don't for - get me, I beg. I re -

mem - ber you said, ___ "Some - times it lasts in love, but some - times it hurts in -

stead." Some - times it lasts in love, but some - times it hurts in - stead.